JEROME VAN KUIKEN

The Creed We Need

NICENE FAITH FOR WESLEYAN WITNESS

ALDERSGATE
PRESS

The Creed We Need
NICENE FAITH FOR WESLEYAN WITNESS

BY JEROME VAN KUIKEN

Copyright © 2025 Jerome Van Kuiken. All rights reserved.

Scripture quotations taken from The Holy Bible, New International Version® NIV®
Copyright © 1973, 1978, 1984, 2011 by Biblica, Inc.
Used with permission. All rights reserved worldwide.

All rights reserved. No part of this book may be reproduced, or stored in a retrieval system or transmitted in any form or by any means, electronic, mechanical, photocopying, recording, scanning or otherwise, except as permitted by the 1976 United States Copyright Act, or with the prior written permission of Aldersgate Press. Requests for permission should be addressed to the editor of Aldersgate Press, *Editor@AldersgatePress.com*.

PUBLISHED BY:
ALDERSGATE **PRESS**
The publications arm of

HOLINESSANDUNITY.ORG

IN COLLABORATION WITH:

lamppostpublishers.com

Printed in the United States of America

Soft Cover ISBN 13:	978-1-60039-315-0
ebook ISBN-13:	978-1-60039-987-9

Contents

Introduction v

1. **ONE FAITH**.. 3

2. **ONE GOD**.. 13

3. **ONE LORD**... 23
   THE LORD IN PERSON

4. **ONE LORD**... 31
   THE LORD IN ACTION

5. **ONE SPIRIT**... 39

6. **ONE BODY**... 49

7. **ONE BAPTISM**... 59

8. **ONE HOPE**... 67

Introduction

Anniversaries matter. Just ask a married couple or a cancer survivor! The year 2025 is the 1700th anniversary of one of the most influential church gatherings of all time, the Council of Nicaea, and its statement of faith, the Nicene Creed. Ever since, this creed has been a touchstone for Christian beliefs. A rule of thumb for testing religious teachings is to ask, *Naughty or Nicene?* It is well worth (re)learning this historic creed. The version used in this book is easily accessible at anglicancompass.com/a-new-creed-the-acnas-revised-translation-of-the-nicene-creed.

The Creed is no independent arbiter of spiritual truth and falsehood, though. It sums up Scripture's witness to God, Christ, and salvation. The Creed's key points echo the apostolic summary of doctrine in Ephesians 4:4–6. We need to review not only the Creed itself but also its biblical basis. The following pages use the 2011 update of the New International Version (NIV).

Along with Scripture and the Creed, this book invites one more guest to the table: John Wesley and the tradition he founded. The reason is not simply that I am in that tradition, but that 2025 is also the 300th anniversary of Wesley's first conversion.

Anniversaries matter! We learn much about faith and life by listening to the three-part harmony of Scripture, Creed, and Wesley.

A brief book like this is an appetizer, not a full banquet. But each chapter ends with recommendations for further reading/viewing. They are ranked from easier reading to harder.

Lastly, 2025 also marks a personal anniversary for me: a quarter century in Christian higher education, much of it at Oklahoma Wesleyan University. I gratefully dedicate this book to OKWU President Jim Dunn, Provost Keri Bostwick, and my dean, Mark Weeter.

The Creed We Need

NICENE FAITH FOR
WESLEYAN WITNESS

chapter one

ONE FAITH

"There is . . . one faith."
Ephesians 4:4–5

"We believe . . ."
Nicene Creed

Dateline: A.D. 325

For the church in the Roman Empire, it was the best of times. Only a few years prior, pagan emperors had tried to annihilate Christianity. Countless believers had lost their lives as martyrs rather than bow to Caesar's gods. Now the new emperor, Constantine, had legalized the religion and summoned its bishops to the city of Nicaea to settle debates over Jesus' identity: what exactly was his relationship to God? Was he a lesser being than God the Father, like a demigod or archangel? That's what a popular preacher named Arius taught. The Council of Nicaea issued a statement of faith for Christians everywhere. It stressed in no uncertain terms that Jesus is just as much God as his heavenly Father is. Arianism was rejected as a false teaching.

A twenty-something Egyptian deacon named Athanasius attended the council. He was short and dark-skinned, so his enemies mocked him as "the Black Dwarf." But Athanasius went on to become a powerful bishop in northern Africa and the chief defender of Nicaea's confession of Christ against those in both church and state who wanted to silence it. Five times he was exiled for his courageous stand, but he never gave up the fight. He kept insisting that unless Jesus Christ—and the Holy Spirit, too—are truly God, then God has not fully bridged the gap to bring us salvation from sin, death, and the devil.

After Athanasius died, the Council of Constantinople (A.D. 381) produced the definitive form of the confession of faith that he had spent his life upholding: the Nicene Creed. It has gone on to become the most agreed-upon Christian creed in history, supplying common ground to believers across nations, generations, and denominations.

Dateline: A.D. 1725

For the church in England, it was the worst of times. Christianity was the official religion, but it was failing to make a practical difference in people's lives. The country's spiritual and moral fiber frayed under the degrading effects of the slave trade, cheap liquor, gambling, sexual immorality, inhumane labor conditions, and public executions and animal cruelty as popular entertainment. Grinding misery reigned among the working class, fashionable unbelief among the elite, and religious anemia among the clergy.

That year, exactly fourteen centuries after Nicaea, a twenty-three-year-old Oxford graduate named John Wesley was preparing for ordination as a deacon in the Church of England. Like Athanasius, he was short of stature and gigantic in later influence. Young Wesley's studies introduced him to the ideal of purity of heart—that the motive behind one's whole life should be to honor God. He fell in love with this vision and straightaway devoted himself to living by it. He spent the next thirteen years vainly attempting to achieve a truly God-pleasing life through his own good works and self-discipline.

Finally, he learned that a right relationship with God is based on personal trust in Christ as Savior. He came to experience that personal trust and assurance of salvation at a religious meeting at Aldersgate in London in 1738. After that, as he preached salvation by faith and God's call to heart purity, revival broke out! People by the droves left lives of sin to follow Jesus. The revival elevated the spiritual and moral tone of the nation as a whole.

Wesley spent the remainder of his life as a traveling evangelist and head of the discipling movement known as Methodism. By the time he died, the movement had morphed into a church, and today is a family of denominations with millions of members around the globe.

The Two Sides of Faith

Today we are 300 years removed from Wesley and the revival in his day. We are 1700 years past Athanasius and Nicaea. Yet they still have much to teach us about *faith*.

The great legacy of Athanasius is the Nicene Creed, a sturdy summary of the core beliefs that bind Christians together whatever their other differences. This is faith as *"the* faith," as when the Apostle Paul writes of "the faith he once tried to destroy" (Galatians 1:23) or Jude refers to "the faith that was once for all entrusted to God's holy people" (Jude 3). It is an objective set of beliefs that we confess together. The very word *creed* comes from the Latin for "I believe," but rather than focusing on my inner experience of believing, a creed outlines what precisely it is that I believe. The related term *orthodoxy* means "right belief." My beliefs are orthodox if they match up with the Creed, which reflects over a millennium and a half of Christian consensus.

For his part, Wesley had something of a love-hate relationship with creed-style faith. He defended orthodox Christianity against the views of those like the Deists, who taught that Jesus was merely a good human religious teacher. He and his lyricist brother Charles published a book of hymns to the Trinity to ingrain in their Methodists the worship of God as Father, Son, and Holy Spirit. But Wesley was also quick to point out the limitations of faith as confession of a creed: even demons believe that there is one God (James 2:19) and that Jesus is his Son (Mark 5:7)! They are perfectly orthodox yet perfectly wicked and lost. Instead, Wesley stressed the subjective side of faith as an act of personally entrusting oneself to God for salvation through Jesus Christ. This is what he experienced at Aldersgate and what he found Scripture celebrating in passages like John 3:16, Romans 4, and Hebrews 11.

In reality, both the *facts* of faith and the *acts* of faith are vital. My leap of faith will end in disaster if indeed there is no ocean at the base of the cliff! But it also does me no good if I have all my facts straight and yet refuse to act on them by taking the dive. The two sides of faith go hand in hand, and each requires the other for us to benefit. Neither dead orthodoxy nor misguided devotion will do. Athanasius cared about sound doctrine not as mere theory or a power trip but because he was convinced that it told the truth that could save the world. Wesley valued personal faith and purehearted devotion to God not for the sake of chasing emotional highs or a generic, customizable spirituality but because he was sure that the true gospel should make a true difference in one's life.

How Wide a Faith?

So far we have looked at Christian faith through the eyes of Athanasius and Wesley. Both of them were men living within Western civilization (though Athanasius was a native Egyptian). This raises a question that takes on some urgency in today's multicultural, egalitarian climate. How relevant are their contributions for women and the world beyond the West?

The short answer is: very relevant. Nicene Christianity was not confined to the Roman Empire in ancient times. It soon spread south to Ethiopia, where it has survived to the present. It crossed the imperial frontier to the east and established itself in Mesopotamia and Persia, then followed the Silk Road toward the sunrise until it reached China in the seventh century. But by the fourteenth century, persecution obliterated the Chinese church along with much of Central Asian Christianity. The rise of Western missions in the modern era has reintroduced the gospel to lands where it once had a home as well as regions where it had never been heard before. Methodists and other heirs of the Wesleyan revival have played their part in world evangelization. The fact that traditional Christianity is flourishing globally even as the West has secularized is a testimony to its multicultural relevance.

Likewise, Nicene and Wesleyan faith have empowered women. After Athanasius, the greatest champions of Nicaea were the Cappadocian Fathers: Basil of Caesarea, his brother Gregory Nyssen, and their friend Gregory Nazianzen. But they in turn held up their female relatives, the "Cappadocian Mothers," as theological teachers and role models of holiness. Roman empresses like Pulcheria, Theodora, and Irene supported Nicene Christianity as well. In later centuries, the Nicene tradition has included female leaders and theologians like Catherine of Siena, Hildegard of

Bingen, Claire of Assisi, Joan of Arc, Teresa of Ávila, and Thérèse of Lisieux.

The Wesleyan movement has encouraged the ministry of women from early on. Wesley's mother Susanna set the precedent by leading parishioners in worship in her ordained husband's absence. Under Wesley's auspices, Sarah Crosby and Mary Bosanquet Fletcher led discipleship groups and preached. The following century saw female evangelists, social reformers, and ministers like Sojourner Truth, Catherine Booth (co-founder of the Salvation Army), Frances Willard, and Anna Howard Shaw. In the twentieth and twenty-first centuries, women rose to the highest levels of denominational leadership as generals (Salvation Army), bishops (United Methodist, African Methodist Episcopal, and Free Methodist Churches), and general superintendents (The Wesleyan Church and the Church of the Nazarene). The faith Athanasius championed and Wesley preached still resonates with millions of women as well as men and in countries throughout the world.

One Faith to Fuel Them All

For the church in today's world, it is the best of times, it is the worst of times. Christianity is the planet's largest religion and growing rapidly in regions like sub-Saharan Africa, East Asia, and Latin America. Yet Christians worldwide endure escalating discrimination and outright persecution at the hands of hostile religions, atheistic regimes, and secular forces of intolerant tolerance. In several countries, the ideology of nationalism seeks to co-opt the church. Debates over sexuality and biblical authority are tearing apart denominations, while repeated scandals of affairs and sexual abuse involving Christian leaders have poisoned the church's reputation in society at large. Unorthodox beliefs about God, Jesus, and salvation are on the rise. What is the church to do?

The Apostle Paul, Bishop Athanasius, and John Wesley would call us back to one faith. It's a faith that:

- *Crosses borders:* The Council of Nicaea came to speak *for* and *to* the worldwide church. Wesley famously claimed that the world was his parish. Christian faith makes us part of a family of believers from every nation, ethnicity, language group, and socioeconomic class, both male and female. Embracing that reality is a crucial step toward undermining racism, sexism, and ethnocentrism while promoting mutual fellowship, accountability, and cooperation in evangelism, discipleship, and relief efforts.

- *Kindles creativity:* The councils of Nicaea and Constantinople innovatively adapted statements of faith from their churches to address the burning theological issues of the day. The result of this creative fidelity was the Nicene Creed, which itself began to be recited and sung as part of public worship. In the Wesleys' era, John innovated by preaching out in the fields where the common people were instead of waiting for them to come to church, while his brother Charles wrote thousands of hymns to share the gospel in a form that people could easily recall and enjoy singing. Today we need the same spirit of creative fidelity to apply sound doctrine to our own pressing theological issues and to communicate the gospel using language, formats, venues, and media that connect with all kinds of people.

- *Sparks revival:* The Wesleyan revival three centuries ago was hardly the last. Revivals have flared up at other times and places since then, from the Second Great Awakening that swept early nineteenth-century America to the Korean Revival of 1907 to the recent Asbury Outpouring in 2023. Where earnest prayer, deep repentance, and single-hearted devotion to God are present, there is revival—or will be in due season.

- *Supports good works and social reform:* After Aldersgate, Wesley knew that good works cannot earn God's favor or replace personal faith in Christ. But he also knew that good works are the natural outflow of genuine faith (Ephesians 2:8–10; James 2:14–26). His Methodist discipleship groups held members accountable to live out their faith by doing good. Some of his own good works were efforts at social reform. For instance, the last letter he wrote was to encourage a young evangelical Member of Parliament, William Wilberforce, in his campaign to end the British slave trade. Wesley compared Wilberforce to Athanasius, who faced down the world to stand for the right. (Incidentally, Athanasius' junior ally Gregory Nyssen was the first Christian to call for the abolition of slavery.) The global scourge of human trafficking, among other social evils, demands a similar faith-filled commitment to good works by contemporary Christians.

- *Enables costly witness:* The martyrs from the years before Constantine found courage to bear witness to Christ even at the sacrifice of their lives. So do the Christian martyrs and all those suffering for their faith still today. Athanasius showed the same backbone in upholding Nicaea's teaching in spite of pressure and sanctions from church leaders and government officials. Wesley likewise kept preaching salvation by faith and the promise of a pure heart even when fellow clergy closed their pulpits to him, the intelligentsia ridiculed him, and mobs assaulted him. We need that holy hutzpah in our own time to avoid keeping quiet or compromising the gospel for fear of peers and authorities.

One faith can do all this. It is one faith for all people and one faith for all seasons. The rest of this book will unpack its rich content.

FOR FURTHER READING/VIEWING

Mark A. Noll, David Komline, and Han-Luen Kantzer Komline, *Turning Points: Decisive Moments in the History of Christianity, 4th edition* (Baker, 2022). This is a handy, non-technical survey of church history, including the Council of Nicaea and the conversion of the Wesley brothers. It also covers the role of women and non-Western Christianity. Start your reading here!

Carla D. Sunberg with Richard Alan Hadley, *Uncommon Virtues: Seven Saints Who Shaped Our Faith* (Foundry, 2018). A popular-level set of studies on the "Cappadocian Mothers" authored by a female General Superintendent of the Church of the Nazarene, with accompanying videos.

Philip Jenkins, *The Lost History of Christianity: The Thousand-Year Golden Age of the Church in the Middle East, Africa, and Asia—and How It Died* (HarperOne, 2008). Anything Jenkins writes is worth reading and easy reading. Here he retells the forgotten story of non-Western Christianity from ancient times to the present and draws lessons for today.

Khaled Anatolios, *Athanasius* (Routledge, 2004). A biography and selection of key writings.

A. Skevington Wood, *The Burning Heart: John Wesley: Evangelist, 2nd edition* (Emeth, 2019). This is a reprint of a classic biography of Wesley. It sets his life and work in the context of England's spiritual and moral crisis. It's not a fast read but well worth the effort.

chapter two

ONE GOD

"There is . . . one God and Father of all, who is over all and through all and in all."
Ephesians 4:4, 6

"We believe in one God, the Father, the Almighty, maker of heaven and earth, of all that is, visible and invisible."
Nicene Creed

Mirrors and Tinted Windows

Listen to people talking on the job, at the park, over a meal, or in the movies, and you will likely hear some reference to "God." They may thank God as a sigh of relief, exclaim about their God as a show of surprise, or call down a curse from God to vent anger or underscore what they are saying. Most of these uses of the word "God" say nothing about whether the speaker believes in God. The word becomes merely a compact mirror that people pull out to reflect their emotions.

At other times when people speak of God, they are serious about it. They may pray. They may discuss what God is like or where God was when bad things happened. But the word "God" may still be a mirror—the full-length size that reflects the speaker's own ideas and wishes. Some lean in close and see someone like themselves, mimicking their own likes and dislikes. We could label this view *just-like-me-theism*. Others stand farther back and see not just themselves but everything around them in the mirror. This outlook is called *pantheism*, the belief that everything is God. Still others have shattered mirrors whose shards reflect many faces. This is *polytheism*, belief in many gods. There are others yet who find the mirror all fogged up, so they conclude that God is unknowable or maybe not even there at all. This view is *agnostic*, meaning "don't know." Then there are *atheists*, who are sure that belief in God is nothing but smoke and mirrors.

But what if a spiritual home improvement expert replaced our mirror with a tinted window—*tinted* because we cannot risk unfiltered exposure to Ultimate Reality, but a *window* so that we can truly see what is out there?

That's what Christians claim happens when God self-reveals. Human thoughts and words about God no longer only reflect their own opinions but begin to relate to the real God. We discover this divine self-revelation particularly and precisely in God's book, the Holy Bible. The Nicene Creed supplies a snapshot of this biblical witness.

Let us see what they show us about God.

God is One

Monotheism is belief in only one God. This belief is shared by Judaism, Christianity, and Islam, and since those last two are the world's largest religions (and growing!), monotheism can seem like just common sense to many people. After all, American currency bears the slogan, "In God We Trust," not "In *Gods* We Trust." But global communication and immigration, as well as the spike in interest in pre-Christian European religions, are making us aware that polytheism is still a live option in today's world.

In the ancient world in which Old Testament Israel was born, polytheism was more than a live option; it was virtually the only game in town. It is a testimony to Israel's influence that monotheism has become the dominant view on the planet, but in the beginning, things were much different. Israel was a small island of monotheism in an ocean of polytheism and always in danger of being swamped by that ocean. Across the Old Testament, God's prophets had to keep warning the Israelites not to worship other gods. These other, false gods were represented by idols (images) that people bowed down to and worshiped. When God gave Israel the Ten Commandments, right at the top of the list was this:

> I am the Lord your God, who brought you out of Egypt, out of the land of slavery. You shall have no other gods before me. You shall not make for yourself an image in the form of anything in heaven above or on the earth beneath or in the waters below. You shall not bow down to them or worship them. (Exodus 20:2–5)

Even in supposedly monotheistic circles today, where no one would dream of bowing down to a literal image, we still face the temptation to serve false gods. Jesus and Paul warned that greed for wealth was idolatry (Matthew 6:24; Ephesians 5:5). Political leaders like Adolf Hitler have followed in the footsteps of pagan kings in the Old Testament (Daniel 3, 6) and Roman emperors in the days of the early church by demanding the total allegiance and devotion that only God deserves. And we still flirt with horoscopes, Ouija boards, Tarot cards, and such.

Moses taught the Israelites that monotheism is meant to be more than an abstract idea. It should be the center around which we organize our whole lives: "Hear, O Israel: The Lord our God, the Lord is one. Love the Lord your God with all your heart and with all your soul and with all your strength" (Deuteronomy 6:4–5). The Ten Commandments sketch out what a lifestyle of single-hearted love for God looks like: We treat God's name with respect. We let God set the tempo of our work and leisure, relying on God to provide our needs. We protect life. We honor our parents and stay faithful to our spouses. We are truthful and trustworthy. We discipline our desires, being grateful for what we have. In these ways we center our individual lives and our life together in community around God, and our unity echoes God's oneness.

God is Father

Moses called on Israel to love God. But that was only after God had taken the initiative in showing love for Israel by delivering the people from slavery in Egypt. As a later writer puts it, "We love because he first loved us" (1 John 4:19). God's love is not just a cosmic energy field of good vibes that we can tap into; rather, God demonstrates love by making conscious decisions to act in specific ways that promote justice and goodness in the world. What that means is that God is a *person*, not an impersonal Force. When Moses encountered God at the burning bush, this is how God self-identified: "I am who I am" (Exodus 3:14). That's a person speaking!

To communicate that God is a person who takes the initiative in loving, the Bible uses the name "Father." Nowadays this name worries some people. Is it insensitive to those who have never known their father? Does it mean that God is a deadbeat or dangerous dad like too many kids have experienced? Could it reinforce the stereotype that women aren't equal to men?

All these questions treat language for God as mirrors instead of tinted windows. They project people's hurts and fears onto God rather than letting God self-reveal using human terms—and redefine those terms in the process! The good news is that God's perfect Fatherhood can heal the wounds left by absent or abusive parents or by chauvinistic males. "Father" was Jesus' favorite name for God, and he taught his disciples to address God the same way (Matthew 6:9). But Jesus revealed the type of Father that God is by forgiving sins, by treating women with respect and as capable of learning and contributing just like his male disciples, and by caring for the lowly and hurting while standing up to the proud and powerful.

The same is true for all the typically masculine language that Scripture uses for God. It does not mean that God is literally male or that women are inferior. It is a tinted window through which God's personhood, initiative, and love shines. Bilquis Sheikh found this out for herself. As a Muslim, "Father" was a forbidden term for God to her. Yet the title of her memoir distills her breakthrough: *I Dared to Call Him Father* (1978). When she prayed to God as Father, she experienced a peace and love that led her to Christ. (We will meet her again in chapter 7.)

God is Almighty

The word for "God" in Hebrew, the original language of the Old Testament, has within itself the idea of being mighty. The gods were thought to have power, which is why people worshiped them. But their powers were limited: each god or goddess had a sphere of authority. There was the god of the sea, the goddess of love, the weather god, and so on. The God of Israel revealed himself as the only true God, whose power and authority are unrestricted. God demonstrated as much when he rescued the Israelite slaves from the mighty Egyptian empire and brought judgment on Egypt's gods by disrupting their domains (the Nile River, the sun, etc.: see Exodus 12:12). Again and again, the Bible celebrates that nothing is impossible for God (Genesis 18:14; Jeremiah 32:17, 27; Luke 1:37; 18:27).

Here again, though, we need to be careful not to turn a tinted window into a mirror. First, every time the Bible says that God can do the impossible, in context it is referring to feats that fit with God's loving and just character. Some things *are* impossible for God because they are out of character for him, like breaking his word (Hebrews 6:18). Second, the fact that God has all power and authority does not mean that we have none. God's sovereignty does not cancel out our freedom. Rather, God's almightiness means that all the might we have, we owe to him. Any ability or say-so we possess is God's gift to us as human beings made in his image (Genesis 1:26–28; Psalm 8), and we are accountable for how we use it.

When tragedy strikes, people often wonder why a loving, almighty God did not step in and put a stop to it. A full answer requires the full creed, including the parts about Jesus' suffering, death, and resurrection and the future Judgment Day and the life to come. Here, though, we are reminded that God has delegated a great deal of freedom and responsibility to created beings (angels, humans, and the world at large), and they can misuse what God has given. But God's love disposes him to have compassion on our sorrows and his power upholds us even in our grief. God's love also guarantees he will act to set things right when he knows it is best. (God's timing is often different from ours.) And God's unmatched authority ensures that when he does act, he can make good on his plans.

God is Creator

God's loving initiative as Father and his power as the Almighty lie behind the creation of the universe. The Nicene Creed recaps Scripture by insisting that absolutely everything—heavenly or earthly, visible or invisible—came into being by God's creative will (Genesis 1:1; Colossians 1:16; Revelation 4:11). Once again, mirror-thinking will mislead us. The universe is not God, as in pantheism. Nor did God create it from pre-existing materials, like a child building a sandcastle. Nor did God himself need to be made by someone or something else. God simply always has existed ("from everlasting to everlasting you are God" – Psalm 90:2) and all else that exists was created from nothing by him.

When the Apostle Paul visited ancient Athens (Acts 17:16–33), he confronted Stoic philosophers who were pantheists and Epicurean philosophers who were a sort of polytheist-atheist hybrid: they thought that the gods ignored humans and that everything on earth happened by chance. Paul tried to switch out their mirrors for tinted windows. He informed them that there is one God who created everything. The true God does not need temples to live in or sacrifices to feed him. But God does not ignore us, either. Instead, God gives us the world to live in and food to eat, and he guides history because he wants us to find him—not for his sake but ours.

God made us from nothing but we're not nothing to him. Nor does he want to be nothing to us even though he wants for nothing.

God is Holy

There is one final word that unites all God is: holy. When God revealed his merciful personhood to Moses at the burning bush, the prophet covered his face and took off his shoes in reverence because he was in a holy zone (Exodus 3:5–6). When God trounced Egypt's gods with plagues, parted the waters, and proved he was in a league of his own, he was displaying his holiness (Exodus 15:11). When he thundered the commandments of monotheism from Mt. Sinai, they came from his holy presence (Exodus 19:9–20:21; Deuteronomy 4:10–20; 5:2–29). When later prophets heard heaven's worship of the Creator, it sounded like this: "Holy, holy, holy" (Isaiah 6:3; Revelation 4:8)!

God's holiness is his utter uniqueness, his set-apartness from all other so-called gods, all limited loves and finite powers, and all of creation. It's why the window of revelation has to have tinting, why Moses hid his face, why Sinai itself shuddered at God's coming.

And yet God *came*. He came to Moses, to Israel in slavery, to Mt. Sinai, to Solomon's Temple, and eventually to a manger in Bethlehem and a cross near Jerusalem. God came because his heart is for us to share in his holiness to the fullest degree possible for finite beings. "Be holy, because I am holy," he calls to us (1 Peter 1:16, quoting Lev. 19:2). His set-apartness is not stay-apartness.

What does it look like for us to reflect God's holiness?

- Because God is *one*, we are to give him undivided loyalty and wholehearted worship (Deuteronomy 6:4–5; 1 John 5:21).

- Because God is fatherly *love* that acts practically and mercifully for our good, we are to love others likewise (Luke 6:27–36; 1 John 3:16–18; 4:7–12).

- Because God is *almighty creator*, we are to trust in his power and use the gifts he has given us responsibly (Matthew 25:14–30; 1 Corinthians 12–14; 2 Corinthians 12:7–10; 1 Peter 4:10–19).

John Wesley would remind us that none of this is possible for us on our own. But the holy God can purify our hearts, fill us with his love and power, and re-create us in his image. Then we will be set apart *from* sin and set apart *for* him. Then we ourselves will be tinted windows through which the light of his holiness shines.

FOR FURTHER READING/VIEWING

In addition to Sheikh's book mentioned above, see the following:

John Mark Comer, *God Has a Name* (Thomas Nelson, 2017). A popular-level study of who God is and what God is like.

John N. Oswalt, *Called to be Holy: A Biblical Perspective* (Warner Press, 2000). A rich but accessible study of God's holiness and ours by a seasoned Old Testament scholar.

Thomas Cahill, *The Gifts of the Jews: How a Tribe of Desert Nomads Changed the Way Everyone Thinks and Feels* (Nan A. Talese/Anchor, 1998). Provocative, sometimes profane, but never boring, Cahill narrates how biblical monotheism changed the world—and still does.

Abdu H. Murray, *Grand Central Question: Answering the Critical Concerns of the Major Worldviews* (InterVarsity, 2014). An ex-Muslim compares the cases for atheism, pantheism, Islam, and Christianity in a thoughtful, readable manner.

Amy Peeler, *Women and the Gender of God* (Eerdmans, 2022). Why Christians call God "Father" when God isn't male, and why that's not bad news for women.

chapter three

ONE LORD
THE LORD IN PERSON

"There is . . . one Lord."

Ephesians 4:4–5

"We believe in one Lord, Jesus Christ, the only-begotten Son of God, eternally begotten of the Father, God from God, Light from Light, true God from true God, begotten, not made, of one Being with the Father; through him all things were made. For us and for our salvation he came down from heaven, was incarnate from the Holy Spirit and the Virgin Mary, and was made man."

Nicene Creed

The Fish of Faith

John's Gospel nears its end with a poignant scene (21:1–7). After the first Easter, seven disciples of Jesus decide to go fishing like they used to do before they started following him. They fish all night without success. Early the next morning, someone on the shore calls out and tells them to cast their net on the other side of the boat. When they do, they catch a miraculous haul of fish. One of the disciples suddenly realizes who's the mysterious figure ashore: "It is the Lord!"

Before Christians used the sign of the cross, they used the sign of the fish. That symbol is still familiar due to its use on business cards and back ends of cars: two arcs (one right side up, the other upside down) that touch at the "head" and cross at the "tail." Some "Jesus fish" now have a cross or the name of Jesus. In the early church, though, the insignia of two overlapping arcs was enough. It recalled stories like John 21 and captured what made Christianity distinct.

Early Christians repurposed the Greek word for "fish," *ichthus*, as an acronym:

- *I – Iesous* (Jesus)

- *Ch – Christos* (Christ)

- *Th – Theou* (God's)

- *U – (H)uios* (Son)

- *S – Soter* (Savior)

To make the sign of the fish was to confess that a Galilean man named Jesus was the Christ, the Son of God, the Savior. The sign of the cross expresses *what he has done* to save us. That's the subject of the next chapter. But the sign of the fish expresses *who he is*. The fish comes first.

Processing the Fish

Every letter of the *ichthus* acronym matters. In the New Testament, Mary and Joseph received angelic instructions to give her baby the name Jesus (Luke 1:31; Matthew 1:21). The name means "The Lord Saves." Here "the Lord" represents the sacred name *Yahweh* that God revealed to Israel (Exodus 3:13–15) to distinguish himself from all other, false deities. He is the God who sent Moses and David, judges and prophets, to free Israel time after time from their enemies. But Jesus would save his people not from foreign foes but from their very own sins (Matthew 1:21).

To do that, he would need to be more than a merely human hero. The Jews had looked for the coming of the Messiah or Christ— both of these titles, drawn from Hebrew and Greek, respectively, meant "Anointed One" and referred to God's specially-appointed leader who would liberate Israel. But Jesus was anointed not by a prophet with holy oil, like past kings of Israel (1 Samuel 10:1; 16:13). Rather, he was anointed by God himself with the Holy Spirit (Matthew 3:16–17).

Previous Israelite kings had been "sons" of God in the sense that they represented God's rule and received God's favor (2 Samuel 7). But for Jesus, being the Son of God meant far more. No man was his biological father. His mother Mary conceived not through sexual relations but by the miraculous power of the Holy Spirit, so that God was his only Father. And his followers came to recognize that Jesus' divine Sonship went farther back than even the start of his earthly life. From all eternity past, God had never been without his unique, "only-begotten" Son, through whom he had created the universe in the first place (John 1:1–18; Colossians 1:15–17; Hebrews 1:1–3).

Because Jesus was the Creator, he could re-create a world gone wrong. As the divine Son, he possessed God's own prerogative to forgive sins (Mark 2:5–12) and raise the dead and judge them (John 5:17–30). Since he had the Holy Spirit like no other, he could cast out demons like no other (Mark 1:21–27; 3:11, 22–30) and fulfill God's promise to give his Spirit to his people so that they would live for him in holiness from the heart (Mark 1:7–8; see Ezekiel 36:25–27). The man from Nazareth was and is the divine Lord, the Savior from sin, death, and the devil.

De-fish-ent Explanations

The claims Jesus and his followers made have been startling and bewildering from the start. How could a man be the one and only uncreated God? How could the one God be Father and Son and Holy Spirit? Trying to make sense of these claims has led to several dead ends called *heresies*.

One popular misconception is that Jesus was *just a good man*—a religious teacher and prophet, maybe even a purely human messiah, but nothing more. In the early church, Jewish believers called Ebionites took this view. In Wesley's era, this was the perspective of the Deists, including Benjamin Franklin and Thomas Jefferson. It persists among liberal Christians, atheists, and Muslims: Islam accepts Jesus as a prophet and messiah but certainly not as God's Son.

Yet diminishing Jesus' identity goes hand in hand with a reduced view of sin. It becomes a mere matter of ignorance or lack of incentive, and the solution is better education. Jesus becomes simply a dispenser of good morals (the Golden Rule, Beatitudes, love commands) and an inspiring example to imitate—a first-century Jewish Gandhi and nothing more. If the problem of evil goes deeper, though, then such a shallow salvation proves inadequate.

A second sidetrack honors Jesus as the first and greatest created being, an archangel or even "a god," but not the eternal, uncreated God. This is the position of Jehovah's Witnesses and their fourth-century predecessors, the Arians. The Council of Nicaea met to address this faulty view. The Nicene Creed rejects the idea that God the Father was ever alone and without his Son: Christ is "eternally begotten of the Father." He is not some lesser god but is just as much God as his Father is: "God from God, . . . true God from true God, . . . of one Being with the Father." And the Creed distinguishes the eternal Son from all created beings: he is "begotten, not made."

Because Jesus shares fully in his Father's deity, he deserves worship and receives prayer just like his Father. Thomas was not committing idolatry when he called Jesus "My Lord and my God!" (John 20:28). Stephen was not sinning when he prayed, "Lord Jesus, receive my spirit" (Acts 7:59). The whole creation is not blaspheming when it gives equal glory to the Father on his throne and the Lamb at his side (Revelation 5:13–14). And because Jesus is as truly God as his Father is, the revelation of God and the salvation that he brings are undiluted (John 14:6–11).

If Jesus and his Father are equally God, yet there is only one God, then are "Father" and "Son" (and "Holy Spirit") just three roles that God plays? This error is *modalism*. It was present in the early church and is still the doctrine of Oneness ("Jesus Only") Pentecostals. The trouble with it is that it does not do justice to the interactions among the three persons of the Trinity that we see in the New Testament. At Jesus' baptism, all three are clearly present simultaneously: the Father announces from heaven that the man coming up from the water is his Son, and the Holy Spirit descends like a dove. Throughout the Gospels, Jesus prays not to himself but to his Father. He even reminisces about how before the world began, he was already receiving love and glory from his Father (John 17:5, 24). And because the one God has always been a communion of interpersonal love, the salvation that Christ brings to us is an invitation to share in that love.

Lastly, once we embrace the fact that Jesus is truly God, it can be easy to lose sight of his true humanity. The church faced a rash of bad theories on this point. Some speculated that Christ had only a divine mind or will or a divinized body instead of a complete, normal human nature, including a human mind and will and a mortal body. But Jesus is as much the son of Mary as he is the Son of God. He had divine authority to do miracles and forgive sins, but he also wrestled with temptation, experienced ignorance, felt hunger, thirst, and grief, fell asleep from exhaustion, and bled and died (e.g., Matthew 4:1–11; 24:36; 26:36–45; Luke 8:23, 45–46; John 4:6–7; 11:33–35; 19:1–37). He lacked nothing of what it is to be God, but he also lacked nothing of what it is to be a human being like us. And because he became like us in every way except sin, he has what it takes to be a sympathetic and sanctifying Savior (Hebrews 2:10–18; 4:15–5:9). He has taken on a complete human nature so that he can redeem and sanctify us completely (1 Thessalonians 5:23).

A Sign of Sound Doctrine

All these heresies (and more!) fail as hypotheses. That does not mean that people who hold these views should be ridiculed or hated, much less burned at the stake! Paul's instructions to Timothy are still valid: "Opponents must be gently instructed, in the hope that God will grant them repentance leading them to a knowledge of the truth" (2 Timothy 2:25). The fact remains that none of these heresies properly accounts for all the truth revealed in Christ. What then? Are we forced into a position of believing in sheer contradictions? God is one. God is three. Jesus is God. Jesus is a man. Are these claims equivalent to talking about square circles and married bachelors?

Thankfully, the answer is no. God is not one *in the same way* that God is three. Jesus is not God *in the same way* that he is a man. When Jesus claimed, "I and the Father are one," he clarified that they were not both the same person: "the Father is in me, and I in the Father" (John 10:30, 38). Within the unity of the one God, there is room for a plurality of persons. That is why the Nicene Creed teaches that the Son is "of one Being with the Father" but not of one *person* with the Father. That is why Paul could rework the classic confession of Jewish monotheism, "The LORD our God, the LORD is one" (Deuteronomy 6:4) to fit in both the Father and the Son: "there is but one God, the Father, from whom all things came and for whom we live; and there is but one Lord, Jesus Christ, through whom all things came and through whom we live" (1 Corinthians 8:6).

The reverse is the case with how Jesus' deity and humanity fit together: within the unity of the one person, Jesus Christ, there is room for both a complete divine nature and a complete human nature. The same person is both the eternal Word who "was with God, and . . . was God" and also "flesh"—that is, human (John 1:1, 14). The same Son is simultaneously "the radiance of God's glory" (recall the Creed: "Light from Light") "and the exact representation of his being" (cue the Nicene "of one Being with the Father") as well as the one who "shared in [our] humanity" and was "made like [us], fully human in every way" (Hebrews 1:3; 2:14, 17).

The sign of the fish illustrates this. It represents two related realities at once: a fish and a belief about Jesus. One and the same emblem has an inseparable double meaning. This *ichthus* = Jesus Christ, God's Son, Savior. It is a fish. And—as in John 21:7—"It is the Lord!"

FOR FURTHER READING/VIEWING

Lee Strobel, *The Case for Christ* (Zondervan, 1998). A classic popular-level introduction to the evidence that Jesus really was (and is) who Christianity claims him to be.

Todd Miles, *Superheroes Can't Save You* (B&H Publishing, 2018). If you're into superheroes, you'll enjoy how the author uses popular culture to explain heresies about Christ.

John N. Oswalt, senior editor, *Holy Love: A Wesleyan Systematic Theology Vol. 1: Christology as Theology* (Francis Asbury Society, 2024). A readable Wesleyan introduction to orthodox Christology (the doctrine of who Christ is).

Jason E. Vickers and Jerome Van Kuiken, general editors, *Methodist Christology: From the Wesleys to the Twenty-first Century* (Wesley's Foundery, 2020). A diverse group of contributors offers a historical survey plus several contemporary proposals—some orthodox, some not.

T. A. Noble, *Christian Theology Vol. 1: The Grace of Our Lord Jesus Christ* (The Foundry, 2022), Parts 1 and 2. The most comprehensive Wesleyan Christology available today, written by an internationally recognized Nazarene theologian.

chapter four

ONE LORD
THE LORD IN ACTION

> "There is . . . one Lord."
> Ephesians 4:4–5

> "For our sake he was crucified under Pontius Pilate; he suffered death and was buried. On the third day he rose again in accordance with the Scriptures; he ascended into heaven and is seated at the right hand of the Father. He will come again in glory to judge the living and the dead, and his kingdom will have no end."
> Nicene Creed

From Agent to Action

Two lines, one sign. In the last chapter we saw how early Christians combined a mirrored pair of curved lines to form a fish sign that expressed their belief about Jesus' *identity*. But put together two straight lines—one vertical, one horizontal—and the result is the sign of the cross, the preeminent symbol of Jesus' *activity*. The two lines of the first sign remind us that Christ unites the divine nature and human nature in his person. The two lines of the second sign symbolize the fact that Christ reconciles the holy God and sinful humanity by his actions. This chapter explores how he accomplishes that at-one-ment (which is where we get the word "atonement"). It lays the groundwork for chapters 6 through 8, which detail how Christ's accomplishment impacts our own past, present, and future.

The Nicene Creed moves immediately from Jesus' birth to his death, from his nativity by his mother Mary to his capital punishment under the Roman governor Pilate. Christ came to save them both and all those like them, and to overcome every human division that they represent. Whether female or male, Jew or Gentile, lowly or powerful, devout or cynical, oppressed or oppressor, all are subject to sin, death, and the devil, and all stand in need of reconciliation with God and one another. The sign of the cross sums up this all-encompassing salvation.

Shadow of the Cross

The Creed skips over the details of Jesus' life between Bethlehem and Calvary, but from the start he lived under the shadow of the cross. He was under two months old when a prophet warned his mother Mary that strife and sword lay ahead (Luke 2:34–35). His

> whole life was one continued scene of misery. No sooner was he born, but he was persecuted by Herod and forced to fly into Egypt in the arms of a weak virgin under the protection of a poor foster father [Matthew 2:13–18]. And when returned into his own country, he for thirty years lived in a low condition, probably employed in the mean trade of a carpenter, which made him in the eyes of the world despicable, of no reputation. And when

after so long an obscurity he appeared unto men, he entered upon his ministry with the severity of forty days abstinence [Matthew 4:1–2].

So wrote John Wesley's mother Susanna in a letter to her children. Doubtless the miseries that Jesus and his parents went through brought her comfort as a minister's wife in an obscure country parish enduring poverty, hostile parishioners, house fires, a poltergeist, frequent childbirth and deaths of children, and sometimes sharp disagreements with her husband. (We will return to this insightful letter in chapter 8.) Jesus' sympathy can comfort us, too, still today.

When he stepped onto the public stage, Jesus identified himself with sinners by standing in line to receive baptism (Matthew 3:13–17). John the Baptist then singled him out as "the Lamb of God, who takes away the sin of the world" (John 1:29). His entire ministry involved bearing his people's ignorance, afflictions, and sins in exchange for the teachings, healings, exorcisms, and forgiveness that he gave (Matthew 4:23–24; 8:16–17). He often taught in parables to test his hearers' hearts, yet he embodied the very mercy, higher righteousness, and perfect love that he preached (Matthew 5–7, 13). As the Holy One of God, he delivered the defiled and excluded by cleansing lepers, expelling unclean spirits, curing a woman's bleeding, eating with sinners, ministering to Gentiles and Samaritans, raising the dead, and redefining cleanliness and Sabbath-keeping to promote purity of heart and abundant living (Matthew 8–9, 12; Mark 7; John 4, 11). He did it all while knowing that his words and deeds would lead to rejection and execution. That is why he taught his disciples that following him meant taking up a cross and laying down their lives for his sake (Luke 9:21–25, 44).

Cross Purposes

As Jesus had foretold, his ministry ended in his betrayal, arrest, sentencing, mocking, scourging, and crucifixion. But how exactly did his suffering produce our salvation? The New Testament gives a variety of overlapping answers, such as:

- Jesus' death was a *ransom* that purchased our freedom (Mark 10:45).

- His death was a *sin offering* that wiped out our guilt (John 1:29; Romans 3:25; 1 Peter 2:24; 1 John 2:2; 4:10; compare Isaiah 53:4–11).

- He *set an example* for us of freedom from sin and faithfulness to God under temptation and unjust treatment (Matthew 4:1–11; Hebrews 2:18; 12:1–3; 1 Peter 2:19–22; 1 John 2:29; 3:3, 5–6).

- His obedience unto death *reversed* Adam's disobedience, bringing righteousness and life for humanity just as Adam brought us condemnation and death (Romans 5:12–21).

- His dying *demonstrates God's justice and love* toward us (Romans 3:25–26; 5:8; 1 John 4:9–10).

- His crucifixion *broke the devil's power* over us (Colossians 2:15; Hebrews 2:14–15; Revelation 12:10–11).

Later generations of Christians have used these biblical materials to build full-scale models of the mechanics of Christ's atonement. As in chapter 2, so also here the metaphor of tinted windows applies. Each model sheds some light on the atonement. But stare too hard at the pane and you are apt to see your own reflection rather than what is on the other side of the glass.

For instance, Jesus' death certainly exemplifies a nonretaliatory love for enemies and exposes the corruption of political and legal systems that kill the innocent. But if that was all that Jesus did, then he would be no better than Socrates, Gandhi, Martin Luther King Jr., or Óscar Romero. His death must be more than a martyrdom.

Likewise, Jesus served as a substitute for Barabbas by undergoing the death penalty in his place (Matthew 27:15–26). Jesus also endured a sense of godforsakenness (Matthew 27:46) and came under the curse of the Law of Moses by dying on a cross (Galatians 3:13). Paul put it starkly: "God made him who had no sin to be sin for us, so that in him we might become the righteousness of God" (2 Corinthians 5:21). But we should not pit the Father against the Son in the work of atonement, as if one cares only for justice and the other cares only for mercy or as if God the Father was an angry, abusive parent looking for someone to hit and Jesus intervened to take the blows for us. Rather, the Father and the Son worked together to provide atonement out of their shared love for sinners (John 3:16) and shared hatred of creation-wrecking sin (Revelation 6:16–17).

Lastly, biblical language about how the cross frees us from slavery to the devil cannot on the one hand be dismissed as sheer superstition. The current revival of interest in the occult reminds us of what the church has always known: there is a supernatural dimension to evil as well as good. Nor on the other hand does it mean that the Evil One is God's equal or that we lack responsibility for our own wrongdoing. We and the spiritual forces of evil stand together as finite creatures in rebellion against the infinite Creator. In faithful mercy, God has chosen to reclaim fallen creation. And in the incarnate Son he has done so by making himself vulnerable to us, absorbing the worst we could do to him, and converting the very means of our refusal of him into the basis of our acceptance by him. That is what happened at the cross. And that is why an instrument of imperial torture, shame, and slaughter has become the preeminent symbol of divine grace and salvation.

God has made of our barricade a bridge.

On from the Cross

The story does not stop on Good Friday, however. After Jesus' death and burial came his resurrection from the dead and his ascension to heaven. These are not optional "bonus features" but are integral to our salvation. Christ's resurrection shattered the power of death and vindicated his claims about himself. Many philosophers and religious teachers have spoken of what may lie beyond death, but only one has returned from the grave as the living guarantee of what the future holds. As Paul insisted, if Christ has not risen from the dead, then we have no release from our sins, no hope for the afterlife, and no reason to trust the apostles as eyewitnesses (1 Corinthians 15).

Forty days after Easter, Jesus ascended into heaven (Acts 1:1–9). This event marked his inauguration as the king of the universe who rules in the midst of his enemies (Psalm 110:1; 1 Corinthians 15:25–26; Ephesians 1:20–23). The first sign of that reign came ten days later when Jesus gave the Holy Spirit to the church at Pentecost (Acts 2). Ever since then, he has led his people by the Spirit, purifying their hearts and empowering them to be his witnesses to the ends of the earth. Not only is Jesus presently reigning as king, he is also interceding as the ultimate high priest and advocate, constantly praying for his once-for-all atonement to be applied continually to our lives (Romans 8:34; Hebrews 4:14–16; 7:23–28; 1 John 2:1).

In the end, Jesus will return to earth to finalize salvation (Hebrews 9:27–28). His second coming will be the reversal of his ascension (Acts 1:10–11). He will descend from heaven in glory to raise the dead, gather his people to himself, and judge the world with perfect justice (Matthew 25; John 5:21–29; 1 Corinthians 15:20–28; 2 Corinthians 5:10; 1 Thessalonians 4:13–5:10). The one who will judge all humans, both the living and the dead, is himself not only God but also a human being who has lived and died and lives again (Romans 14:9; Revelation 1:18). His reappearance will abolish sin, death, and the forces of evil fully and forever from God's good creation (1 Corinthians 15:24–28; 2 Peter 3; Revelation 20–22). At last, the holy reunion that the cross signifies—the vertical and the horizontal, God and humanity, heaven and earth—will be complete.

FOR FURTHER READING/VIEWING

Edgardo Colón-Emeric and Mark Gorman, *The Saving Mysteries of Jesus Christ: A Christology in the Wesleyan Tradition* (Cascade, 2019). Survey of Christ's life. Includes discussion questions.

Joshua M. McNall, *How Jesus Saves: Atonement for Ordinary People* (Zondervan, 2023). A popular-level survey of the doctrine of the atonement with companion videos. (For a more advanced but still very readable discussion, see *The Mosaic of Atonement* [Zondervan, 2019] by the same author, also with companion videos.)

Thomas H. McCall, *Forsaken: The Trinity and the Cross, and Why It Matters* (InterVarsity, 2012). A short book on how the Trinity and the atonement go together.

Charles Wallace Jr., ed., *Susanna Wesley: The Complete Writings* (New York: Oxford University Press, 1997). The authoritative source. The letter to her children is on pages 377–407.

T. A. Noble, *Christian Theology Vol. 1: The Grace of Our Lord Jesus Christ* (The Foundry, 2022), Part 3. Comprehensive coverage of the saving work of Christ from a Wesleyan stance.

chapter five

ONE SPIRIT

"There is . . . one Spirit."
Ephesians 4:4

"We believe in the Holy Spirit, the Lord, the giver of life, who proceeds from the Father [and the Son], who with the Father and the Son is worshiped and glorified, who has spoken through the prophets."
Nicene Creed

The Big Bang

It all began with a burst of light and a blast of wind. On July 16, 1945, the scientists of the Manhattan Project detonated the world's first nuclear device on a testing ground in the New Mexico desert. That explosion set off a new era with an unprecedented energy source available for human use. It could heat entire cities or incinerate them. It could supply reliable, cheap, and clean electricity or fuel an unpredictable, costly arms race and contaminate the planet with radiation. Light and darkness, life and death: these are what a single event on a summer day ushered in. The Jewish physicist in charge of the test understood its significance. Robert Oppenheimer code-named it "Trinity."

Nearly two millennia beforehand, an even more epochal event released a far greater power into the world. A rush of wind in a crowded room, the flash of tongues of flame igniting overhead, the sudden outburst of praise to God in languages unlearned—together they signaled the Holy Spirit's arrival on the day of Pentecost (Acts 2:1–4). Here was the power that Jesus' disciples had lacked during his earthly ministry, the power he had told them to await in Jerusalem until it came, the power that would enable them to carry the gospel to the ends of the earth (Acts 1:1–8). The rest of the book of Acts and of the New Testament demonstrates how light and darkness, life and death follow in the wake of the Spirit's activity: as the gospel goes forth into all the world, those who accept its illumination find new life in the Spirit, while those who shut their eyes and harden their hearts to it condemn themselves to destruction. And with the coming of the Holy Spirit, God completes his self-revelation as the Trinity.

The Nicene Creed retraces this pattern of revelation by confessing faith in the Holy Spirit after the Father and the Son. The Creed associates the Spirit with three titles (Holy Spirit, Lord, life-giver) and three actions (proceeds from God, receives worship with and as God, has spoken through prophets). Wesleyanism and its younger sisters, the Pentecostal and Charismatic Movements, have paid great attention to the Holy Spirit. Still, it is worth revisiting the ancient church's wisdom on the subject to ensure that we are balanced in our beliefs and spiritual experiences. This chapter teases out the meaning of the Spirit's creedal titles and actions.

More Than a Force

We learn first that the Spirit is a *person*, not merely a *power*. The Creed echoes Scripture by calling the Spirit "Lord"

(2 Corinthians 3:16–18) and telling us that the Spirit speaks (e.g., Hebrews 3:7; Revelation 2:7, 11, 17, 29; 22:17). "Lord" is a title that *persons* have and speaking is what *persons* do, especially when the one speaking uses "I" and "me" language (see Acts 13:2). Even though the name "Holy Spirit" is not as overtly personal as "Father" and "Son," it too can have the flavor of personhood. The older English translation of the Spirit's name as "Holy Ghost" brought out this nuance—ghosts are thought of as personal beings, not impersonal. Unfortunately, that translation carries with it unwanted connotations of haunting and horror that undermine its positive features.

The New Testament displays the Holy Spirit's personhood. Jesus promises "another advocate" like himself who will take up the task of teaching once Jesus has left for heaven (John 14:16–17, 26; 15:26; 16:7). Peter rebukes an early Christian couple for lying to and testing the Holy Spirit (Acts 5:3, 9). A church council claims that the Spirit joined its deliberations: "It seemed good to the Holy Spirit and to us . . ." (Acts 15:28). Paul writes that the Spirit groans in prayer for us and that God the Father knows the Spirit's mind (Romans 8:26–27). Other letters warn against grieving or insulting the Spirit (Ephesians 4:30; Hebrews 10:29). These are all personal qualities. One cannot lie to electricity. Magnetism has no mind. Gravity neither groans nor grieves.

Why, though, does the Holy Spirit have a less relatable-sounding name than the Father and the Son? Why do the Spirit's symbols (fire, water, wind, a dove) tend to come from nature rather than from human society? Perhaps one reason is to keep reminding us of the mysterious otherness of God. Even more than nuclear energy, God is beyond our understanding and control. Maybe another reason is that the Spirit always points away from himself, not to himself: "he will testify about me," Jesus explains (John 15:26).

Like John the Baptist, who was filled with the Holy Spirit from his mother's womb (Luke 1:15), the Spirit's testimony is ever, "Look, the Lamb of God" (John 1:29, 36) and "He must become greater; I must become less" (John 3:30). Where the Spirit is genuinely at work today in individuals and movements, that same attitude prevails.

Greater Than an Angel

The Holy Spirit is not just a power but a person. The Spirit is also not just *good*, but *God*. During the time of Athanasius and the debate over Nicene theology, there were some who were willing to accept that Jesus was God just like God the Father is, but they balked at recognizing the Holy Spirit as God. They preferred to see the Spirit as one of the many angelic spirits that God had created. This same view of the Spirit cropped up later in Islam: Muslims tend to identify the Holy Spirit with the angel Gabriel. The Creed pushes against this perspective in several ways:

- It gives the Holy Spirit the divine title "Lord," the same title given to Jesus to identify him with the one God of Israel (see chapter 3).

- It speaks of the Spirit's origin in terms of *proceeding* from God rather than *being made*.

- It insists that the Spirit is equally worthy of worship and glorification alongside the Father and the Son.

Let us explore more of the biblical evidence that upholds the Creed's claims.

Already in the Old Testament, the Spirit of God shares in God's perfect wisdom and knowledge (Isaiah 40:13–14), inescapable presence (Psalm 139:7–10), and almighty power (Isaiah 63:11–14; Zechariah 4:6–7). In the New Testament, lying to the Holy Spirit is lying to God (Acts 5:3–4) and the Holy Spirit's temple is God's temple (1 Corinthians 3:16–17; 6:19; Ephesians 2:21–22). Early Christians worship "the Lord," and "the Holy Spirit" replies (Acts 13:2). They pronounce benedictions—which are a form of *prayer*—equally in the name of the God the Father, Jesus Christ, and the Holy Spirit, showing that all three are equally the one God of Israel (2 Corinthians 13:14; Revelation 1:4–5; the "seven spirits" here alludes to Isaiah 11:2's sevenfold description of the Spirit of the Lord). They baptize in the one name (that is, the one divine identity) shared equally by Father, Son, and Holy Spirit (Matthew 28:19). Again and again, they coordinate all three in the one work of salvation (e.g., 1 Corinthians 12:4–6; Ephesians 1:3–14, 17; 3:14–17; 1 Peter 1:2).

Holy Spirit, Holy Trinity

This consistent threefold pattern in Scripture does not mean that the three persons of the Trinity are purely interchangeable or that they are simply three roles that the one God plays in the world (that is the heresy of modalism, which we discussed in chapter 3). Rather, all God's works come *from* the Father *through* the Son *in* the Holy Spirit's perfecting power. This pattern of divine activity in history reflects the eternal pattern of God's inner life: the Son is eternally *begotten* of the Father, while the Holy Spirit, in the words of John 15:26, eternally *proceeds* or "goes out from the Father" of the Son. Here the church stretches biblical language as far as it will go to express the conviction that God is not utterly different in himself than he is toward us but that God is forever a dynamic, lifegiving communion of interpersonal love.

Tragically, this stretching of biblical language led to a breaking point between the Eastern and Western wings of the church a thousand years ago. The original Nicene Creed said only that the Spirit "proceeds from the Father," harking back to John 15:26. Centuries later, the church in the West added the single Latin term *filioque* ("and the Son") to stress Jesus' relationship to the Spirit. But unlike the original Nicene Creed, no ecumenical church council had approved this change of wording. The pope tried to impose it on his own authority, but the church in the East refused to accept it. In A.D. 1054, the church split into the Eastern Orthodox Church on the one hand and the Roman Catholic Church on the other. When the Reformation broke out in the sixteenth century, Protestant denominations inherited the *filioque* from Catholicism. Only with the rise of ecumenical discussions between East and West in the twentieth century has there been progress in healing the rift caused by the *filioque*.

One lesson from the *filioque* fiasco relates especially to Wesleyans, Pentecostals, and Charismatics: do not divide the Spirit from the Son. Whatever works of grace or spiritual gifts the Spirit brings are because of Christ, are meant to glorify Christ, and should encourage Christlikeness. Anything that diminishes or distracts from the Son dishonors the whole Trinity.

Spirit of Life

The Creed names the Father as the "maker of heaven and earth" and the Son as the one "through [whom] all things were made." The comparable label for the Holy Spirit is "giver of life." Not only does this title nod to New Testament descriptions of the Spirit

(John 6:63; 1 Corinthians 15:45), but it also reflects pivotal movements of the Spirit across Scripture. At the fountainhead of creation, the Spirit of the Lord hovered above the unformed world's dark waters to bring forth light, order, and life (Genesis 1). The Spirit continues to enliven new generations of creatures throughout time and space (Psalm 104:27–30). The prophet Ezekiel predicted that someday the Spirit of God would fill God's people to revive them from their state of sin and death (Ezekiel 36:26–27; 37:1–14).

That prophecy began to come true through Jesus. The Holy Spirit overshadowed Mary to bring forth life from her virgin womb (Luke 1:34–35). At the opposite end of Jesus' earthly career, the Spirit raised him from the dead as the prototype of our future resurrection (Romans 8:11). Even now, Christ gives us a new birth and eternal life through his Spirit (John 3:5–8; Romans 8:1–16). But we are not to remain spiritual infants. The life-giving Spirit grants spiritual gifts and grace so that the collective body of Christ may grow up in salvation and reach spiritual adulthood, the fullness of life in Christ (1 Corinthians 12–14; Ephesians 3:14–4:16; 1 Peter 1:22–2:5; 4:10–11).

The Speaking Spirit

The Creed focuses on one specific spiritual gift, the gift of prophecy, by confessing that the Holy Spirit "has spoken through the prophets." The next section of the Creed will refer to the apostles as the founding fathers of the church, so the prophets in mind here are the ones whose writings became the Old Testament, just as the apostles' testimony became the New Testament. Today the Old Testament suffers from neglect, abuse, and scorn. Many both outside and inside the church are ignorant of it. Outspoken atheists have ridiculed it. Prominent megachurch pastors have called for Christians to "unhitch" from it altogether or break up its contents into "buckets" of the good, the bad, and the obsolete. But both Jesus and his apostles saw the whole Old Testament as prophetically pointing toward himself under the inspiration of the Spirit (Luke 24:44; John 5:39; Acts 3:21–25; 2 Timothy 3:16; 1 Peter 1:10–12; 2 Peter 1:19–21). The Holy Spirit ensures that Holy Scripture is true and trustworthy in its testimony.

Although the Creed does not mention it, the same Spirit who spoke through the prophets still speaks through Scripture, sermons, wise words from both believers and unbelievers, and the inner witness of the Spirit in our hearts (see, e.g., John 11:49–52; Romans 8:15–16; 15:4; 1 Peter 4:11). How can we tell if it is the Spirit of God speaking or a lying spirit (or even the fabrication of our own imagination or indigestion)? Scripture offers us these tests:

- Does it line up with sound doctrine? False teaching will deny core beliefs like the one God of Israel (Deuteronomy 13:1–5); Jesus as Lord and Christ who has come in the flesh (1 Corinthians 12:3; 1 John 4:1–3); salvation by faith, not works of the law (Galatians 1–6); and the resurrection of the dead (1 Corinthians 15; 2 Timothy 2:17–18).

- Does it produce the fruit of godliness and good works or sinful living or even simple confusion (Matthew 7:15–20; 1 Corinthians 14:26–33; Jude)?

- If predictions are made, do they come true (Deuteronomy 18:20–22; Isaiah 44–46)?

Over the course of church history, many false prophets and false teachers have appeared and have gained large followings. Their adherents run in the millions yet to this day. It is vital to discern the difference between the Spirit of truth and spiritual tricksters.

Bigger Than a Bang

Ever since Pentecost, the church has had available to it the power of the Holy Spirit. Unlike the nuclear power unleashed by the 1945 Trinity test, this power is *personal*, not an impersonal force, and it is *divine*, not a finite, creaturely capability. These qualities keep the Holy Spirit from being manipulable by us or subject to laws beyond himself, like a chemical in a test tube or a genie in a bottle. They also mean that the Spirit is not random and irrational like a force of nature. His will and reasons may be mysterious to us, but he is gracious, not capricious. The Spirit's power is *life-giving* and *truth-delivering*. We may depend on him not to deceive or destroy us as we follow his lead by faith. In all these ways, he is indeed the *Holy* Spirit.

FOR FURTHER READING/VIEWING

Beth Felker Jones, *God the Spirit: Introducing Pneumatology in Wesleyan and Ecumenical Perspective* (Cascade, 2014). A short survey on the Holy Spirit by a Wesleyan theologian. She covers both the doctrine's history and its current expressions. Good for group studies.

Fred Sanders, *The Holy Spirit: An Introduction* (Crossway, 2023). Another short survey of the doctrine of the Holy Spirit by a Wesleyan theologian. He focuses on classic Protestant sources.

Thomas Smail, "The Holy Spirit in the Holy Trinity," in Christopher R. Seitz, ed., *Nicene Christianity: The Future for a New Ecumenism* (Brazos, 2001), 154–165. A clear, concise summary of the *filioque* debate, why it matters, and what the solution could be.

Jeffrey W. Barbeau and Beth Felker Jones, eds., *Spirit of God: Christian Renewal in the Community of Faith* (IVP Academic, 2015). A smorgasbord of studies on the Holy Spirit.

Oliver D. Crisp and Fred Sanders, eds., *The Third Person of the Trinity: Explorations in Constructive Dogmatics* (Zondervan, 2020). Another diverse collection of Holy Spirit studies by an international cast of contributors.

chapter six

ONE BODY

"There is one body."
Ephesians 4:4

"We believe in one holy catholic and apostolic Church."
Nicene Creed

Body Building

The cosmos and its inhabitants came from a body. This explanation of origins was widespread in olden times. Norse poets sang of how the giant Ymir's corpse turned into the world. In China, a similar legend spoke of Pan Gu as the cadaver behind creation, adding that humans were descendants of the parasites living in his flesh. The Mesopotamian epic *Enuma Elish* recorded how Marduk, patron deity of Babylon, split in half the carcass of the monstrous goddess Tiamat to form the heavens and earth, then used the remains of Tiamat's slain consort Kingu to fashion humankind to be the gods' slaves. According to Hindu scripture, the distinct castes of people sprang from various parts of the god Brahma's body: priests from his head, warriors from his arms, merchants from his belly and loins, and manual laborers from his feet. (The outcaste untouchables emerged from the ground beneath Brahma's heels.)

The Apostle Paul, too, used a body to describe the origins and organization of the church. But for him, believers were not a giant's flea-spawn or Frankenstein slaves or factions distinguished by a descending scale of value. Rather, the Son of God in his own crucified and risen flesh had demolished the divisions between Jew and Gentile, enslaved and free, male and female, incorporating them all as distinct but equally valued members of a new humanity headed by himself—the church, the body of Christ (1 Corinthians 12:12–27; Galatians 3:28; Ephesians 1:22–23; 2:14–16). The Holy Spirit animates this body and equips its members for growth and service, and so both Ephesians 4:4 and the Nicene Creed place the Spirit and the church side by side.

The Creed identifies a quartet of marks to distinguish the true church, the authentic body of Christ, from imposters. As Jesus had prayed for his disciples to be united, sanctified, equipped with his whole teaching for the whole world, and sent forth into it (John 17), so the church is one, holy, catholic, and apostolic. John Wesley adapted these four marks to the early Methodist movement so as to further the Spirit's work of revival. This chapter examines the marks of the church and Wesley's adaptation of them, as well as their readaptation in our own time.

The One-Body Problem

The very first mark of the church appears to be utterly at odds with reality. Whatever organizational unity the church may have enjoyed when the Nicene Creed was composed has long since disintegrated. By the fifth century, Christians who agreed on the Creed nevertheless had split into three rival groups over differing explanations of how Jesus could be simultaneously fully God and fully human: the "miaphysites" in Africa, India, Syria, and Armenia; members of the Church of the East in Mesopotamia, Persia, and farther east; and the Chalcedonians, mainly in Europe. Then in A.D. 1054, the *filioque* controversy fractured the Chalcedonians themselves into Roman Catholics and Eastern Orthodox. In the sixteenth century, the Reformation separated Protestant churches from the Roman Catholic Church, and their number has only multiplied until today there is a dizzying diversity of denominations, nondenominational churches, and interdenominational organizations that operate under the banner of Christianity. How can anyone today recite with a straight face, "We believe in one . . . Church"?

Here the biblical history of Israel may help us. At times, the Israelites were institutionally unified, such as under Moses' leadership in the Exodus or under Kings Saul, David, and Solomon in Canaan. But there were also long stretches of time when each tribe functioned independently (the Judges era) or Israel was divided between northern and southern monarchies (2 Samuel 2–4; 1 Kings 12; 2 Kings 17) or sects like the Pharisees, Sadducees, Zealots, and Essenes competed for the people's allegiance (the New Testament era). And yet for all these variations in governance and grouping, the Israelites retained their identity as a single people, marked off from all others by bloodline, history, and covenant. That heritage still binds today's Jews together despite the divisions within modern Judaism.

In a similar manner, the oneness of the church depends not on a single institutional structure but on a shared (new) covenant, history, and spiritual connection to Christ our Head and to one another as joint members of his body (1 Corinthians 12). Wesley himself saw the one true church as the fellowship of all those who, regardless of denomination, share one living faith and hope in the one God and the one Lord Jesus by means of the one Holy Spirit (Ephesians 4:4–6). That is why he collaborated with Calvinists in evangelism, commended Catholic saints as models of sanctity, and scheduled Methodist meetings so as not to conflict with Anglican church services.

The same recognition of common ground has borne ecumenical fruit especially since the mid-twentieth century. Chalcedonian and non-Chalcedonian communions have revisited their old disputes and determined the problem to be about language and church politics, not actual heresy. Eastern and Western scholars are making strides to resolve the *filioque* feud. Catholics and Protestants have agreed on the basics of the doctrine of justification (how we are put right with God). Christians across denominations cooperate in world evangelism, Bible translation, disaster relief, religious liberty, the protection of the unborn, and opposition to injustices like slavery and genocide. As fractious as the Christian family may be, it remains "one body" (Ephesians 4:4).

A Sanctified Body

If confessing the oneness of the church seems to contradict the evidence, so too does pledging faith in the holiness of the church. Hypocrisy and heinous misdeeds by self-identifying Christians regularly make the news. Ironically, though, the very standards by which the world often weighs the church and finds it wanting are drawn from the church. Those who condemn Christian complicity in violence, imperialism, sexual misconduct, superstition, and oppression of the poor and the "other" are borrowing their moral yardstick from Christianity's incalculable influence on the development of international law, politics, ethics, science, education, and healthcare. That influence derives ultimately from the Founder of the faith, who minted the term "hypocrite" for his religious opponents; preached nonretaliation; demanded both outward and inward sexual integrity; keenly observed and delighted in nature as his

Father's handiwork; showed compassion for the needy and countercultural respect for women, children, and foreigners; and spurned earthly power and prestige, sacrificing himself for others instead.

While Christ is singularly sinless and holy, he died to make his church holy, clean and unblemished (Ephesians 5:25–27). Wesley stressed that the sanctifying Spirit channels holiness to those united to their Lord by faith. The Methodist movement aimed to aid believers' pursuit of holiness of heart and life through spiritual disciplines and group discipleship. Wesley held together the gracious, uncoerced work of the Holy Spirit and the responsibility of human beings to seek holiness, grow in grace, and live out a godly life. Over the past several decades, evangelicals in the West have rediscovered the spiritual disciplines and have developed a host of discipleship resources, including parachurch ministries like the Navigators, Bible Study Fellowship, Renovaré, Promise Keepers, and Celebrate Recovery. Contemporary Methodists are even retrieving Wesley's "class meetings" and "bands" as corporate discipleship structures. Meanwhile, pan-Wesleyan organizations like the Wesleyan Holiness Connection, the Holiness Partnership, and the Francis Asbury Society promote the message of the Holy Spirit's supernatural gift of sanctifying grace to those who believe.

The Breadth of the Body

The third creedal mark is catholicity. At the root of this term is *wholeness*. The classic slogan "The whole gospel for the whole world" captures the dual emphasis of this mark. On the one hand, the church is responsible to proclaim "the whole will of God" (Acts 20:27), not just the popular or easily understood parts of the gospel. Wesley did not hesitate to preach *both* justification *and* sanctification, *both* salvation by grace through faith *and* the importance of good works. In interpreting and applying Scripture, he appealed to church tradition *and* reason *and* spiritual experience. He sought to save souls *and* educate minds *and* promote health in bodies, all for the sake of loving his neighbor as himself.

On the other hand, the church must extend the gospel's invitation to the whole world, regardless of gender, ethnicity, nationality, social or economic status, or any other factor (Matthew 28:19; Galatians 3:28). Wesley claimed the world as his parish, meaning that he would go wherever sinners needed the gospel. He preached in the fields where the unchurched were. Both women and men, both the working class and the well-to-do, both persons of African extraction as well as those of European descent were included in his Methodist groups. He also advocated a "catholic spirit" that could recognize those from different denominations and traditions as fellow Christians and cooperate with them, provided only that they agreed on the basics of the gospel.

Catholicity is the crucial complement of unity. A church that is one but not catholic constricts into a narrow sectarianism in which the only true Christians are those who look or think exactly like me. Catholicity celebrates the full range of doctrines, spiritual gifts (1 Corinthians 12; Ephesians 4:7–16), and human differences that are compatible with the truth of the gospel. Boundaries of orthodoxy there still will be, but they are set by the broad consensus of the historic and global church, not by some small segment of it. The contemporary expressions of the church's oneness described earlier in this chapter are simultaneously signs of catholicity.

A Body Sent and Steadfast

If the church is to reach the whole world, then it must send out heralds to announce the good news of salvation. And if their announcement is to be reliable, then it must align with the teaching of Christ's original disciples, the eyewitnesses he himself authorized to testify to the gospel throughout all nations (Matthew 28:19). These authorized representatives of Christ were the *apostles*, meaning "sent ones." For the church to be apostolic means that it holds true to the mission and message of the first apostles, on whose testimony the church is founded (Matthew 16:16–18; Luke 1:1–4; Galatians 1:11–2:9; Ephesians 2:19–20; Hebrews 2:3). Their authoritative testimony is preserved for all succeeding generations in the New Testament. It is by the Scriptures, then, that the church's fidelity to its apostolic calling must be judged.

Wesley not only traveled throughout the British Isles as an itinerant evangelist and overseer of Methodist discipleship groups; he also commissioned others, including lay preachers in England and superintendents (soon to be called bishops) for the Methodists in America. His spiritual heirs have spread the gospel across the globe. While in the past the movement of the church's mission went from the West to the rest of the world, today flourishing churches in Asia, Africa, and South America are sending abroad their own witnesses for Christ. Likewise, Christian leaders from outside the West are holding European, North American, and Australian churches to account for drifting from apostolic faith and practice. Where catholic consensus and apostolic accountability are ignored, the church's holiness and unity cannot survive.

The Three-Body Solution

One event above all concretely concentrates the church's four marks: the Lord's Supper. Paul sees it as symbolizing *unity*: "Because there is one loaf, we, who are many, are one body" (1 Corinthians 10:17). He warns against violating the *holiness* of the Lord's table through idol feasts (1 Corinthians 10) or its *catholicity* by discriminating against the poor and behaving selfishly (1 Corinthians 11:17–22, 27–34). And he anchors the practice of Holy Communion in the *apostolic* memory of the Last Supper, when Jesus himself instituted a continuing commemoration of his sacrificed body and out-spilled blood (1 Corinthians 11:23–26). By some mysterious, much-mooted manner, in the Eucharist three bodies converge: Christ's flesh on the cross, Christ's bread on the table, Christ's people around it. Ancient mythmakers dreamed that we and our world came from a body—one perhaps dead, perhaps divine. In the Lord's Supper, we taste the truth.

FOR FURTHER READING/VIEWING

In addition to Noll's and Jenkins' books listed at the end of chapter 1 and the websites of the organizations named in this chapter, see the following:

John Wesley, Sermons 39: "Catholic Spirit" and 74: "Of the Church," easily accessible at *wesley.nnu.edu/john-wesley/the-sermons-of-john-wesley-1872-edition*. This website hosts a wealth of material by and about John Wesley and other early Methodists.

Tom Holland, *Dominion: How the Christian Revolution Remade the World* (Basic Books, 2019). A sympathetic atheist historian recounts how deep a debt Western civilization owes Christianity.

Kevin M. Watson, *Doctrine, Spirit and Discipline: A History of the Wesleyan Tradition in the United States* (Zondervan, 2024). The author of previous books on Wesleyan discipleship (*The Class Meeting; A Blueprint for Discipleship*) and the Spirit's gift of sanctification (*Perfect Love*) here traces the whole history of Methodism and the Wesleyan Holiness Movement in the USA.

Tom Greggs, *Dogmatic Ecclesiology* (Baker, 2019 and forthcoming). A thorough three-volume doctrine of the church by a Methodist ecumenist. Volume 1 is presently available.

chapter seven

ONE BAPTISM

"There is . . . one baptism."
Ephesians 4:4–5

"We acknowledge one Baptism for the forgiveness of sins."
Nicene Creed

A Stir in the Waters

An ex-Klansman being baptized by an African American preacher—that's the striking scene that encapsulates *Burden*, the biography by Courtney Hargrave and the film by the same title (both 2018). Both relate the true story of how in Laurens, South Carolina, Reverend David Kennedy played good Samaritan to Mike Burden, a known KKK member down on his luck. The practical compassion that the reverend and his congregation showed led to Mike's conversion to Christ. In the waters of baptism, he buried his burden of guilt, washed away his old identity as a violent racist, and rose up to a fresh start in life.

A Pakistani Muslim immersing herself in her bathtub to end the squabbles among her Christian acquaintances over the right way to baptize her into their faith: that's one telling episode in Bilquis Sheikh's autobiography *I Dared to Call Him Father*. It exposes the irony that the "one baptism" (Ephesians 4:5) meant as a source of unity for believers has become a matter of contention. When, why, how, and even whether to baptize are points of dispute even in Wesleyan circles. But as Bilquis, Mike, and the Creed remind us, baptism has some relation to new life in Christ—that is, *conversion*. And Wesleyans who are true to their evangelical roots can agree that conversion is vital, regardless of precisely how baptism links to it.

This chapter takes up Christian conversion and its connections to the Wesleyan way of salvation as a whole; to the spiritual discipline of forgiving others; and in between, to baptism. First, though, a word on the creedal sequence of topics: it may seem backwards to have covered the body of Christ before the individual believer's experience; sanctification and mission before conversion; and the Lord's Supper before baptism. But the Creed's order poses a challenge to the self-centeredness at the heart of our sinful condition. Instead of beginning with my wishes and felt needs, it reorients my thinking outside of myself by prioritizing the Trinity and the church. Only by being embedded in the communion of the saints with the triune God and one another can I find the life, peace, and meaning that I was made for. The Creed advertises this grand vision first, then informs me how to gain access to it through Christian conversion.

This is the Way

The Creed itself leaps straight from the start of the Christian life ("one Baptism for the forgiveness of sins") to the finish ("the resurrection of the dead, and the life of the world to come"). Here is where Wesley and his heirs help to flesh out the creedal bare-bones account. The Wesleyan view of conversion sees it as a *crucial* event but not an *isolated* one. Conversion is an important moment in the overall *way* (or *order*) of salvation. The word "salvation" takes in the entire spiritual journey of the Christian from beginning to end, not simply one milestone (however significant) along the route. Here is how Wesleyans map out the way of salvation:

- *Predestination* (Romans 8:29; Ephesians 1:4–6, 11–12) – God has designed and built the highway of salvation, setting up in advance ("pre") where it will lead ("destination") and establishing the rules of the road. God did all this without our input or assistance.

- *Prevenient grace* (John 6:44–45; 12:32; 16:8; Acts 17:25–28; Romans 1:19–20; 2:14–15) – This is the "on ramp" to the highway of salvation. God is constantly at work in everyone, providing for them, enabling them to recognize and desire what is good and true, convicting them of sin, and drawing them toward Christ to be saved.

- *Conversion* (Luke 24:47; John 3:3; Romans 4:1–5:2; 8:15–16; Titus 3:4–7) – This is the "merging lane." God grants those convicted of sin the grace of *repentance* (turning from their sins) and *faith* (turning to Christ as Savior). In response, several things occur at once: God *forgives* their sins, *justifies* them (declares them to be in right relationship with himself), and *regenerates* them (causes them to be "born again" spiritually). New converts know all this has happened because the Holy Spirit gives them a sense of inner assurance that they now belong to God's family (this is called *the witness of the Spirit*).

- *Sanctification* (Romans 6:19–22; 2 Corinthians 6:14–7:1; 1 Thessalonians 5:23–24; Hebrews 12:7–14) – Converts spend their lives traveling on the way of salvation, developing into experienced spiritual motorists as they learn to pay attention to the highway signs; avoid road rage, distracted driving, and the potholes of sin; and keep pressing forward through sunny and stormy weather alike. But Wesley trusted that God can bring repentant believers into a condition of *entire sanctification*, in which the pure love of God and neighbor fully directs one's life. It is in some sense like driving in the fast lane: the journey is far from over, driver error and even breakdowns are still possible, but there is freedom from being slowed down by lesser loves and selfish stubbornness.

- *Glorification* (Romans 8:18–25, 30; Philippians 3:20–21) – This is the destination we have driven toward and dreamed of since the start, and it lies across the state line from this earthly life. Christ will grant his faithful people immortal, perfected life in his presence forever. We will fully reflect the image of our sinless, glorious, resurrected Lord.

Surveying the layout of the way of salvation allows us to gain our bearings on conversion. As pivotal as it is, it is not the whole story. Our roadmap also supplies background information necessary for a generously Wesleyan view of baptism. We wade into that subject next.

The Ways of Water

Coming from an Anglican home, Wesley believed that infants were "born again" in baptism but that most of them backslid as they grew up and so needed to be born again *again* by accepting Christ for themselves. Mainstream Methodism after Wesley has kept infant baptism but sees it less as the moment of regeneration than as initiation into the church family, with a later personal commitment to Christ (sometimes formalized through confirmation or reaffirmation of baptismal vows). Various Holiness Movement churches have adopted the Baptist practice of believers' baptism as a convert's public testimony, sometimes insisting on full immersion rather than sprinkling or pouring as the only legitimate baptism. Yet these churches also dedicate infants. Holiness Quakers and the Salvation Army have gone even further by treating water baptism as optional at best and at worst replacing salvation by grace through faith with reliance on mere ritual (though Salvationists do dedicate infants and have swearing-in ceremonies for their soldiers). The "one baptism" that counts is the outpouring of the Holy Spirit into a convert's life.

When we consult the Bible for guidance, we find variety, not uniformity. John the Baptist offered "a baptism of repentance for the forgiveness of sins" in which people would confess their sins, be baptized, and receive forgiveness in a single event (Mark 1:4–5). John's baptism thus functioned like a revival service's "altar call," when people come to the front of the sanctuary or stadium and pray to be saved. On the first Christian Pentecost, Peter repeated

John's call to repent and be baptized for forgiveness, with the added promise of the gift of the Holy Spirit (Acts 2:38). Yet Jesus forgave people without baptizing them (Luke 5:17–26; 7:36–50; 19:1–10; 23:40–43) and some converts received the Holy Spirit before being baptized (Acts 10:44–48; 11:13–17). All the above cases involve adults, but Paul baptized whole households (Acts 16:14–15, 29–34; 1 Corinthians 1:16). Did that include infants? Interpretations differ. We do find biblical precedent for the dedication of small children (1 Samuel 1:24–25; Matthew 19:13–15; Luke 2:22–24).

The Wesleyan way of salvation allows us to incorporate the variety of biblical and historical practices into the progress of grace in human lives. Infant baptism or dedication hails the prevenient grace that grants a child the opportunity—and its family and congregation the duty—of a Christian upbringing. Confirmation, reaffirmation of baptismal vows, or believers' baptism may coincide with converting grace in those old enough to choose Christ themselves. For those who first convert and later are baptized in obedience to Christ, baptism becomes a sign and means of sanctifying grace. Those who refrain from baptism as a prophetic protest against dead ritualism may also be following the leading of the sanctifying Spirit, just as biblical prophets performed disruptive sign-acts (e.g., Isaiah 20:2–4; Jeremiah 19; Ezekiel 4), so long as they allow for the Spirit's ability to make of baptism itself a prophetic sign-act and means of grace.

As for the proper method of baptism, the use of the Jordan River (John 3:23) and the imagery of burial, the Red Sea crossing, and Noah's Flood (Romans 6:3–4; 1 Corinthians 10:2; Colossians 2:12; 1 Peter 3:20–21) certainly suggest immersion. But Scripture also uses sprinkling (Ezekiel 36:25–27; Hebrews 10:22) and pouring (Isaiah 44:3; Titus 3:5–6) as symbols of being cleansed from sin and receiving the Spirit. The scarcity of water in desert regions led an early church manual called the *Didache* to recommend pouring water three times over the head of the person being baptized if water was in short supply (*Didache* 7:3). It would seem, then, that immersion is the *preferable* but not *exclusively valid* mode of baptism. Again, the Wesleyan way permits diversity of practice so long as there is evidence of God's transforming grace at work in a person.

Passing the Pardon

Out of the treasury of biblical word-pictures and descriptions of how Christ's atonement impacts us, the Creed singles out forgiveness. Yet that selection has implications not only for conversion, when we first receive God's forgiveness, but also for a lifetime of sanctification. Jesus taught his disciples to make a habit of praying for divine forgiveness, and he linked it to our practice of passing along forgiveness to others (Matthew 6:12, 14–15; 18:21–35; see also Ephesians 4:32). If we refuse to forgive those who wrong us, we cannot expect God to forgive our wrongs against him.

But forgiving others is a spiritual *discipline*, not something that comes easily, costs little, or depends on our feelings. Nor does it simply ignore or excuse wrongdoing or require that we automatically trust the offending party. What it does mean is that we make the hard choice to extend the same grace that God has shown to us by seeking the wrongdoer's good. That is what Reverend Kennedy did by helping out a Klansman in spite of parishioners' suspicions and his own anger at everything Mike Burden stood for. Practiced wisely and well, forgiveness has incredible redemptive power. It has altered the course of entire nations. It certainly changed Mike's life. Experiencing a Christian's forgiveness led him to seek Christ's forgiveness and literally take the plunge into a new life—a life claimed by "one Lord, one faith, one baptism" (Ephesians 4:5). May our lives, too, bear the well-watered fruit of forgiveness.

FOR FURTHER READING/VIEWING

Phil Tallon and Justus Hunter, *The Absolute Basics of the Wesleyan Way* (Seedbed, 2020). A beginner's guide to Wesley and the Wesleyan way of salvation with companion videos.

Desmond Tutu, *No Future Without Forgiveness* (Image, 2000). Methodist-turned-Anglican Archbishop Tutu led nonviolent resistance to South African Apartheid. Once it ended, he chaired the Truth and Reconciliation Commission, which applied the Christian principle of forgiveness on a national scale. This is his unflinching yet hopeful testimonial.

M. William Ury, *The Bearer: Forgiving As Christ* (Teleios, 2015). A Wesleyan study of the Christian discipline of forgiveness.

Jonathan A. Powers, general ed., *New Life in the Risen Christ: A Wesleyan Theology of Baptism* (Cascade, 2023). A diverse collection of essays, though omitting Quaker/Salvation Army views.

Jerome Van Kuiken, ed., *Reclaiming the Order of Salvation: Evangelical Wesleyan Perspectives* (Francis Asbury Society, 2025). Contributors explain and defend the Wesleyan way of salvation.

chapter eight

ONE HOPE

"There is . . . the one hope of your calling."
Ephesians 4:4

"We look for the resurrection of the dead,
and the life of the world to come."
Nicene Creed

A Hope to Hold to

Susanna Wesley was worried about her children. Almost a year ago a fire had burned down their home at night. They had barely escaped with their lives—none more so than her five-year-old son John, whom neighbors had snatched through an upstairs window just as the flaming roof fell in! Now, eleven months later, the children were still living with neighbors while the parsonage was being rebuilt. Susanna fretted about their spiritual condition in her absence. They needed training in godliness, and it was her duty to see to it. On January 13, 1710, she wrote them a letter that would serve as a catechism, a brief guide to the Christian faith, based on the Apostles' Creed. When she came to the passage on the resurrection of the dead, she stressed that God will reverse every effect of decomposition. The children could look forward to their bodies being restored just like their rebuilt parsonage.

Gregory Nyssen, whose family carried forward Athanasius' mission to establish the Nicene Creed, was reeling with grief. The name "Athanasius" might mean "Immortal," but he and those who followed in his footsteps still died. Gregory had missed his brother Basil's funeral, finally making it back home in A.D. 379 only to find his elder sister Macrina on her own deathbed. But Macrina would tolerate no tears from Gregory. She launched into a heady discussion on Scripture and philosophy with him, reminding her theologian brother that this earthly life and mortal body are not all there is; there is eternal life and resurrection to come. After her passing, he wrote up a biography of his sister and teacher, along with a transcript of their dialogue, *On the Soul and the Resurrection*.

Whether in the first, the fourth, the eighteenth, or the twenty-first centuries, the same hope has bound believers together in every generation: *resurrection*. Its firm foundation is the rising again from the dead of Jesus Christ himself. The Apostle Paul spends an entire chapter (1 Corinthians 15) arguing against those who thought that they could be Christians while denying the resurrection of the dead. Without that doctrine, Paul warns, the whole gospel collapses, and we are left without hope of eternal life, without forgiveness for our sins, without a Savior who truly has triumphed over sin and death, and without a reason to do more than chase fleeting pleasures before we pass away forever. This final chapter focuses on that ultimate hope.

Better Than Heaven, More Real Than Reincarnation

The hope held out by Bible and Creed differs from popular (mis)conceptions about the afterlife. Against secularism, it affirms that there actually is an afterlife. But the promised resurrection is not simply our souls going to heaven when we die. Scripture occasionally touches on that idea (Luke 16:19–31; 23:43; Philippians 1:21–24; Revelation 6:6–11), but its emphasis is not on our flying away to heaven but on Christ's descending from there someday to transform our mortal bodies into images of his immortal body (1 Corinthians 15:42–57; Philippians 3:20–21; 1 Thessalonians 4:13–18). What will happen to our bodies will affect the whole of creation as well: the cosmos will be freed from sin, death, and decay, and renewed into a holy habitation where God dwells with his people forever (Romans 8:18–25; 2 Peter 3:13; Revelation 21–22). The meek really will inherit the earth (Matthew 5:5).

If resurrection is more than merely going to heaven, neither is it equivalent to reincarnation. Christianity does not teach that our souls keep being reborn into different temporary bodies until we offload our karma. Rather, God has created us as individuals with a body that is uniquely our own, and this is the same body that our Savior will reconstitute and bring to everlasting perfection when he raises the dead. No karma can override Christ's present word of forgiveness or his future command to come forth from the grave!

The negative goal of reincarnation is to finally free oneself from being tied down to a body. In Buddhism, this goal goes along with another: release from any sense of a distinct, desiring self. In New Age spirituality and its Hindu counterpart, the goal is loftier: to experience absolute oneness with God and all things. That ambition harmonizes with the view known as pantheism, which we covered in chapter 2. By contrast, creedal Christianity assures us that:

- *Personhood is permanent* — Neither death itself nor nirvana afterwards spells the end of your distinctive self.

- *Matter matters* — Who you uniquely are includes your body; the proper goal is not to free you from it but to free it from death.

- *God is greater* — God cannot be equated with the world or the human self. God always remains greater than the created order. But because God is a person (indeed, three persons!), not merely a force, God willingly, graciously enters into loving and righteous relationship with creation. Our aim must be not the impossible dream of *being* God but rather of *being with* God forever.

Hope and Hard Questions

All the dead will rise again. But that "all" includes both the righteous and the wicked (Daniel 12:2; John 5:28–29; Acts 24:15–16). No one will be left out of Christ's summons to rise, stand before him, and receive commendation or condemnation (Matthew 25:31–46; 2 Corinthians 5:10; Revelation 20:11–15). Those who have suffered exploitation and oppression will finally get justice. Those who have quietly, faithfully done right will receive public praise. Those who have coddled secret sins will conceal them no longer. Those who have brazenly defied God will find no place to hide from his judgment. And all those who have taken refuge in the Son of God will be blessed (Psalm 2:12).

Biblical teaching about the resurrection and judgment of the dead leaves questions that Christians have debated for centuries.

What about those who have never heard the gospel or whose understanding of it is deficient? Is there a purgatory in the afterlife for believers who die before they are completely sinless? What exactly is the nature of hell? Will everyone eventually be saved? Speaking broadly, the following perspectives fit best with a Wesleyan viewpoint:

- The Father desires all to be saved; Christ died for all; the Holy Spirit works for the salvation of all, even beyond the church's reach (John 3:16–17; 12:32; 16:8; Acts 17:27–28; Romans 5:18; 2 Corinthians 5:14–20; 1 Timothy 2:3–6; Hebrews 2:9; 2 Peter 3:9). Only those who reject or neglect God's grace are finally lost (Matthew 25; John 3:18; Hebrews 2:1–3; 3:7–4:11; 6:4–8; 10:26–31; 2 Peter 2; Jude).

- God does not coerce anyone to be saved, nor does God guarantee a person's future salvation apart from ongoing obedient faith. Wesleyans historically have rejected notions that God unconditionally predestines individuals to be saved or that onetime believers are eternally secure ("Once saved, always saved"), which would also rule out the doctrine that everyone will certainly be saved in the end.

- An eternity estranged from God is the worst fate imaginable, and Scripture uses a variety of graphic images to get that point across. We should not get so caught up in the details that we miss their main point.

- God works instantaneously to put believers right with him (justification), bring them to life spiritually (the new birth), fully devote them to himself (entire sanctification), and transform their bodies from mortal to immortal (glorification). No prolonged purgatorial experience, therefore, seems necessary in the afterlife.

How Should We Then Live?

In light of Christian hope for the hereafter, how should we live in the here and now? First, we should not become too attached to the things of this life or too distressed when we lose them. Christ and his apostles warn against worry, the love of earthly pleasures and treasures, and despair in the face of death and difficulties (Matthew 6:19–34; 13:1–23; 1 Thessalonians 4:13; 1 Timothy 6:6–10; 1 Peter 4:12–19; 1 John 2:15–17). Rather, our focus must stay fixed on preparing ourselves and others for what will last forever: the coming unshakable kingdom of God.

Secondly, this does not excuse being lazy or wasteful with our present duties, bodies, or environs. Jesus' parables of talents, sheep, and goats and Paul's rebuke of slackers alert us that God expects us to stay busy and act responsibly (Matthew 25:14–46; 2 Thessalonians 3:6–15). We are stewards of our time, money, and possessions, along with our very bodies and planet, and will answer to God for what we have done with them. In an economy of personalized consumerism, we must invest in community and in what reflects goodness, truth, and God's glory. In a society that cheers on self-expression and self-definition even when it mars bodies and spreads disease and confusion, we must act with truth, justice, and compassion. In a society likewise spiking in self-harm and suicide, we must help all persons find a dignity drawn from their Maker and Redeemer. In an ecology blighted by pollution and overconsumption, we must care for creation.

Lastly, a genuinely Christian hope gives birth to present peace and joy. Whatever sorrows and setbacks we may go through in the short term, the long-range forecast is bright with promise. As Paul, himself no stranger to struggle and suffering, put it: "our light and momentary troubles are achieving for us an eternal glory that far outweighs them all" (2 Corinthians 4:17). This attitude has strengthened Christian martyrs from ancient times until now. It also made the early Methodists famous for their deathbed testimonies. Neighbors, family members, and friends who watched loved ones die with patience amid great pain, with singing hymns instead of complaining and cursing, and with confidence in eternal life (and sometimes even with visions of heaven) were eyewitnesses to Christ's victory over sin and death. May we set a similar example today!

For the people of Israel facing foreign invasion, Isaiah painted a prophetic portrait of a future beyond all catastrophe, when God will punish proud oppressors, give relief to the poor, invite every nation to feast at his table, and terminate death's reign forever by emptying every tomb in a great resurrection event (Isaiah 24–26). So too the author of Hebrews envisioned how all who have lived as pilgrims in this present age, placing their faith and hope in a lasting city not built by human hands, will gather in the city of God for a festival with the saints and martyrs of the ages, hosts of angels, and the glorious presence of God and his Son (Hebrews 11–12). Here are comfort and joy enough for family funerals in the fourth century, homeless children in the eighteenth century, and us amid war, pandemic, and ordinary difficulties today. Here is hope!

FOR FURTHER READING/VIEWING/LISTENING

In addition to Sunberg's book on Macrina and her family listed at the end of chapter 1, Murray's worldview book from chapter 2, and Susanna Wesley's letter from chapter 4, see the following:

Christine Johnson, "Holiness and Death in the Theology of John Wesley," *Thrive* podcast, *thrive.asburyseminary.edu/dr-christine-johnson-holiness-and-death-in-the-theology-of-john-wesley*. Johnson discusses her PhD research on "holy dying" in early Methodism.

N. T. Wright, *Surprised by Hope: Rethinking Heaven, the Resurrection, and the Mission of the Church* (HarperOne, 2018). Why resurrection—Christ's, ours, the whole creation's—matters.

Preston Sprinkle, general ed., *Four Views on Hell, 2nd edition* (Zondervan, 2016). Evenhanded evangelical coverage of the main options on hell, as well as purgatory.

Timothy C. Tennent, *For the Body: Recovering a Theology of Gender, Sexuality, and the Human Body* (Zondervan, 2020). A Wesleyan theology of the body.

Howard A. Snyder with Joel Scandrett, *Salvation Means Creation Healed: The Ecology of Sin and Grace: Overcoming the Divorce between Earth and Heaven* (Cascade, 2011). A Wesleyan call to embrace the ecological implications of salvation.